# Ann

1820 - 1878

Sally Grant

**The Larks Press**
Pocket Biographies No. 9

Printed and published by

The Larks Press
Ordnance Farmhouse
Guist Bottom, Dereham, Norfolk
NR20 5PF

01328 829207

British Library Cataloguing-in-Publication Data
A catalogue record for this book is available
from the British Library

Copyright - Sally Grant 1996
ISBN 0 948400 41 2

# ANNA SEWELL

1820-1878

*Black Beauty* was Anna Sewell's only attempt at writing, and yet it has sold 30,000,000 copies and is the sixth bestseller in the English language.

Anna Sewell was born, at 25, Church Plain, Great Yarmouth, in the Market Place, squashed between St Nicholas Church (England's largest parish church) and a 17th century almshouse for needy fishermen.

It was a small, narrow, three-storied house, one room above another, with an enclosed yard and kitchen and washroom behind. At the other end of the market, was grandfather William Sewell's large grocer's shop.

Yarmouth, with its noisy coasters, fleets of black-sailed wherries, and barrels of salted herrings rattling along quays, was an exciting town. There were shrimp parlours and smoke houses for curing kippers wedged between tall old merchant houses; longshoremen brought cockles, crabs, whelks, herring, sprats and mackerel for market.

Mary and Isaac Sewell, Anna's parents, were plain Quakers and adopted their distinctive form of dress and speech. The men wore large brimmed hats, and the women long sober-coloured gowns, with low necklines and full sleeves. A soft crowned bonnet with stiff muslin brim, curving around the face, was tied beneath the chin.

Dancing, music, theatre outings and other 'idle pursuits' were frowned on. Friends addressed each other as Thee, and Thou, and weekdays were numbered not named. Shaking hands was undesirable, Mr and Mrs abandoned and Christmas was not celebrated

Anna's father was a partner in a small draper's shop, but soon after her birth, Isaac Sewell was having trouble making ends meet. He left for London, opening a shop in Bishopsgate selling Quaker clothes. Mary took Anna to her parents' home, Felthorpe Farm, owned by Quaker cousins John and Ann Wright of Buxton in Norfolk, then farmed by Mary's brother John.

In 1813, grandfather John Wright had become involved in a steam ferry service between Norwich and Yarmouth. But, three years before Anna's birth, his packet had exploded killing thirteen passengers. Anna's mother remembered that her father had seen the bodies 'laid side by side in the Foundry garden close by the river side', and that 'the streets were so thickly packed that a ball might be rolled across their heads.' Grandfather's fortune had gone on compensation.

Felthorpe farm, which played an important part in Anna's childhood, was about 800 acres of rather poor land, described by Anna's biographer, Susan Chitty, as 'half heath and woodland, and the remainder a poor sandy soil, that had been reclaimed from heath. The trees were mostly oak and Scotch fir' - the first planted in Norfolk for timber. John Wright kept sheep, for which it was ideal, and livestock, riding to Holkham Hall, twenty miles distant, for the sheep shearing.

Isaac meanwhile had bought a small house in Camomile Street, close to Spitalfields and was converting it into a shop from which he would sell Quaker clothing.. It was the first time Mary had left Norfolk, and she loathed London, with its 'fog, dirt, noise, and distraction' - and the gin palace opposite the house.

> 'Drunk for a penny
> Dead drunk for tuppence.'

The shop did not thrive, and they moved to Hackney, where Anna's brother Phillip was born. Isaac entered into partnership in a new shop, but the enterprise ended abruptly, when he was declared bankrupt. Furniture and wedding presents went to pay his debts, and he became a traveller in Nottingham lace, renting a house at Dalston.

An early oil painting of Anna aged sixteen, shows a thick-set, square, determined girl, with rich, thick, curly hair, serious expression, broad brow and turned up nose. Girls at this time wore low-necked, short-sleeved dresses, long frilly trousers and white socks. This portrait of Anna shows her similarly dressed in a frock exposing neck and shoulders, edged with frills and a gathered bodice.

Dalston then was at the very edge of London, and 12, Park Road, was at the centre of a red brick terrace. Isaac left at 8 in the morning, and returned at 8 in the evening. Neighbours lived quiet lives. Remembering her childhood, Mary took 'Nanny' and Phillip to the lanes and fields behind the house, collecting flowers and insects, which they drew before they let them go. Improving poems played a part in their education:

> Love yourself last my darling,
> Be gentle and kind and true,
> True to yourself and others,
> As God is true to you.'
> (*Little Miss Marigold.*)

In later years Mary herself would contribute:

> My mother says that we may learn
> From e'en the smallest thing,
> That all God's creatures everywhere
> A useful lesson bring.
> (*The Children of Summerbrook*)

The Sewells had just one maidservant and life was simple, with 'porridge thick and hot', and lessons with Mary who had very decided views on the upbringing and education of children. She followed closely the principles of Richard and Maria Edgeworth.

'At stated times', Mary wrote to a friend, 'the child should be set up at the table to amuse itself quietly,...Children should not be accustomed to too much variety; they do not need it...A child will amuse itself for

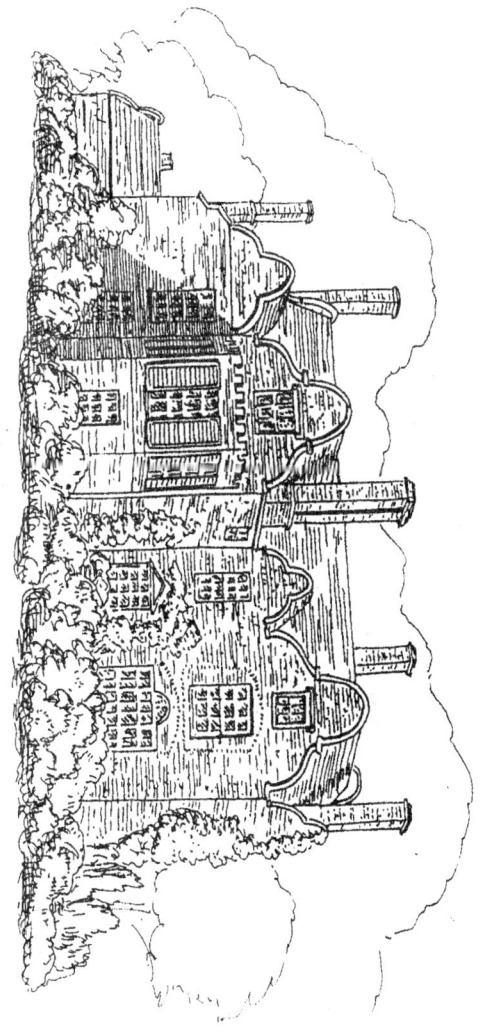

Dudwick House in Anna's time, believed to have been the model for Birtwick Park, Black Beauty's first working home
Drawing by David Yaxley

a very long time in stringing beads,...drawing, cutting etc. ...Perfect play is the anticipation of perfect work. It is surprising how soon a child will accommodate itself to... a routine, if it be invincibly regular.'

Anna was taught thrift and honesty and good plain sewing and Mary was especially firm about kindness to all God's creatures. Things did not always go as planned. On Anna's ninth birthday Mary wrote that she 'is much disposed to idle over lessons and work. She needs to get the habit of a cheerful surrender of her own will - to give up entirely telling tales of her brother. She begins to be useful to her mother, but is not tidy.'

Among this stifling disapproval, there was one ray of hope. 'She has a great deal of courage and independence of character, never burdened with fear.' When a neighbour shot a blackbird - it was Anna who flew into a fury. 'No' she said, 'thee cruel man, thee shan't have it at all.'

Summers were spent at Buxton, with days at Yarmouth, smelling of 'fish, pitch, oakum, and tar.' Anna caught the stage coach from Whitechapel, for the 17-hour journey to Buxton. Cousin Wright's eighteenth-century farmhouse, Dudwick House (replaced by the present Dudwick Hall in 1939) is thought to have been Anna's model for Black Beauty's first home. The stables, surrounding a courtyard, entered through imposing stone-balled pillars, still go by the name of 'Black Beauty's Stables.' Anna's grandparents had been installed at Home

Farm, and it is probable she stayed here, acquiring her love of horses when she learnt to ride Balaam, who drew the chaise.

'The first place I remember was a large pleasant meadow with a pond of clear water. Some shady trees leant over it, and rushes and water-lilies grew at the deep end. Over the hedge on one side we looked into a ploughed field, and on the other into our master's house. At the top of the meadow was a plantation of fir trees, and at the bottom, a running brook overhung by a steep bank.' (*Black Beauty*, Chapter 1.)

When Anna was 12, Isaac accepted a loan from an uncle, a Norfolk miller, to buy Palatine House, a converted coach house at Stoke Newington. Anna attended school for the first time. The house had an orchard and meadows, and Mary kept cows, pigs, ducks and bees - and bought a rabbit hutch. Much of the work was done by Anna and Philip. But it was at Palatine House that Anna's life changed.

Returning from school, she was caught in a thunderstorm and began running. The drive to the garden sloped sharply, the wet grass was slippery, and she fell awkwardly, 'spraining her ankle.' But in those disastrous seconds, she must have done greater damage, as she became a semi-invalid for the rest of her life, unable to walk properly and virtually crippled. Anna doesn't mention pain in hips or legs, but an 'inability to walk after the accident.' Possibly a break, healing badly, put strain on the rest of her body. But for long periods she could not walk at all. From an active lifestyle, she was reduced to constant frustration. Anna Sewell began the dreary life of many Victorian women - tethered to a sofa.

The family moved to Brighton in 1836 and Isaac became the first manager of the Brighton branch of the London and County Joint Stock Bank. Anna and her mother loathed the fashionable life of Brighton. Crippled in her early twenties, surrounded by smart, fashionable people, she must have felt genuine misery, with little hope of marriage, home or children. She did not inhabit, or wish to, the world of calling cards (with their corners neatly turned, and an unwritten law of 30 minute calls, with cups of tea and slices of Madeira.)

Walking was difficult. Like her own creation, Black Beauty, she knew the constant fear of falling:

'When the streets were slippery with frost or snow, that was the worst. One mile of such travelling, and no firm footing, would take more out of us than four on a good road; every nerve and muscle of our bodies was strained to keep our balance. The fear of falling is more exhausting than anything else.' *(Black Beauty.)*

There were problems of faith also while in Brighton. Mary Sewell had already left the Society of Friends in favour of the Evangelical movement which embraced 'justification by faith'. Anna went through her own spiritual crisis from which she eventually found relief in the Church of England.

Nevertheless, both Anna and her mother were very active socially in Brighton. Mary was tireless in visiting the poor; Anna became a Sunday School teacher and learnt to play the piano. She and her brother Philip, whom she adored, went to lectures and sermons and began to have their own friends.

The Sewells moved to Lancing, and bought a pony and trap. This move was followed by several others within the county of Sussex while Isaac continued to work at the bank. The pony was an important part of Anna's life and she became particularly skilled at driving the trap, 'quickly detecting if anything is wrong with a horse's foot, and through her eye she knows at once if anything annoys them' as her mother later wrote. Philip married Sarah Woods and became a railway engineer. His career and travels in Spain were followed with great interest by Anna.

When she was able and still hopeful of improving her health, Anna visited spas, and in 1846 was well enough to visit Marienbad with Philip. When she returned, Isaac had done the unthinkable and become a brewer. Undoubtedly this caused family strife for Mary became a temperance worker and Philip later refused £10,000 for a small plot of land rather than have it used for a pub. Eventually Isaac returned to banking, and bought a

*Anna Sewell from an early photograph
Drawing by Robert Yaxley*

house in Chichester. During Anna's absence Mary, at the age of 60, burst into verse with *Homely Ballads For The Working Men's Fireside*, which was not published until 1858, but proved very popular. Then Isaac was off again to Wick in Gloucestershire.

'On a high hill,..it is healthy and almost as inconvenient as it can be...Our letters every day take two good hours to get and post...the roads almost impassable in parts..' Here Mary continued her writing with Jarrolds as her principal publishers, and Anna took over the management of the household. A visitor to the house wrote: 'The "plain living" which they loved to associate with "high thinking" was marked by exquisite order and nicety, such as one rarely sees.'

The six years in Gloucestershire were calm and productive ones. Mary wrote and Anna established an evening school for the miners and labourers of the district. Then, in 1864, they were off again to Bath, where Isaac had obtained another banking post. Anna liked Bath, but Mary regretted the life they had left.

At this point, in 1867, the whole family went back to Norfolk. More than anything they wished to be near Philip (then in Norwich) whose wife had recently died leaving him with seven children. They bought a small L-shaped red brick house, flanking the Norwich to Aylsham road - the White House at Catton.

'The drawing room was over the dining room,....with

an outlook behind over the garden and the fields beyond it to the village church....The roof of the verandah made a balcony, outside the large back window of the drawing room; there Mrs Sewell trained flowers and creepers in boxes to make a garden for Anna ..' In the garden grew 'flowers of all seasons - primroses, wood-sorrel, speedwell, wild geranium, lilies of the valley, and climbing things full of blossom...' (Mrs Bayly. Visitor.)

Anna's two main interests in these years were her nieces and nephews and the reformatory at Buxton, known as the Red House School which Philip had inherited from Cousin Wright. Every Monday morning Philip would call on his way to Buxton and in the evening he would call out 'Goodnight' as he passed the White House riding on his splendid black mare, Bessie.

Then, in 1870, Philip married again and his children no longer demanded their Aunt's attention. About March 1871 Anna became ill. 'She is usually in bed till midday, and then dresses, resting between whiles. She lies on the sofa for the rest of the day....' The doctor ceased to come, for Dr R. gave 'no hope and was only discouraging.' said Mary. As Anna had a cough and was also 'flushed and animated' one guesses at consumption. And dying, Anna Sewell did an extraordinary thing. Having given up drawing, and shown scant interest in forming verses, she began to write a book!

In her diary for November 6th, 1871 she wrote, 'I am

writing a life of a horse, and getting dolls and boxes ready for Christmas.' It is impossible to know what motivated her. The model for Black Beauty seems to have been Philip's black mare Bessie.

Exhausted, she wrote daily on tiny pieces of paper, which she handed to Mary who took the completed draft to Jarrolds London office. A book whose popularity and worldwide esteem she could never have anticipated, was bought outright by Mr Tillyer, Paternoster Row, for £20. It was published on 24th November 1877 and Anna did not live to see all its success, but it was just beginning to be acclaimed when she contracted her final illness. *Black Beauty* has been claimed by animal-lovers to be a milestone in the understanding of proper treatment for horses. It helped to bring about the abolition of the abominable bearing-rein.

Anna died in April 1878. She was buried in Lamas Quaker burial ground. Imagine Mary Sewell's horror when she saw that the horses in the funeral cortège were all wearing bearing reins. Quietly, but very firmly, she went out and persuaded the men to remove them.

Perhaps in the sensitivity she showed towards the beautiful black horse whose life was ruined by a fall - Anna drew on her own life, that of a strong-minded little girl who had become an unfulfilled invalid. Why she wrote it we will never know, but *courage* was her shining quality, and Nanny Sewell ended, like Black Beauty, a survivor.

## Further Reading about Anna Sewell

*The Woman who wrote Black Beauty*
Susan Chitty